Just a Girl Who Got It All
How You Can Have YOUR All Too
Tanya Bardo

Thank you to my mum and dad who raised me up so that I can stand on mountains.

To my amazing husband Phil for all of your patience and support, I love you more than words can say. Thank you to my three amazing children Gabriella, Rocco and Renz for challenging me daily to practice what I preach.

Thank you to my inspiring best friend Kitty, my amazing supportive sister Sherrie and my whole family for making another one of my dreams come true.

David Lawson, Amanda and Lee at YM Designs and Sharon Emery Creative Arts Professional and Writer in Residence at St Mary's Centre.

Contents

Introduction

A brief note about this book.

When I first showed my husband Phil the title of this book, he didn't like it. He said it made me sound big-headed, as if I had landed on my feet and wanted to show off. I explained that when I was a young single mum with no money I came across an article about the power of positive thinking, which said I could be or do anything I wanted in my life.

I had always wanted to be a model, travelling the world and being on the front covers of magazines, earning lots of money for my daughter Gabriella to have a nice life.

Before I read about the power of positive thinking I never believed I would become a model as I'm only

5'3' and I was sure there were millions of girls who were better looking. But the article intrigued me and I became obsessed with reading personal development books and began to apply the techniques I read about to my life. Some of them worked for me, and some didn't but within a year I went from being a single mum with no money to a well-known model travelling the world. I featured on numerous front covers of magazines and appeared in adverts and TV shows worldwide. I was able to provide for me, and my daughter through doing a job I loved - my dream had come true!

After seven years of modelling I started to yearn to fall in love with someone special, have more children and a big happy family home. So I applied the same techniques I'd used to land my dream job and voilà, I met my Phil and we have two perfect, healthy and happy boys together and a wonderful big family home.

After 10 years of studying and researching everything I could to do with self-help, I became a life coach helping others lead their dream life.

Now I would like you to understand that when I say I have got it all I mean that I have got everything I want in life. My idea of an ideal life might be the complete opposite to yours but it doesn't matter; the techniques work for whatever you want in life.

I didn't get anything in my life by accident, I dreamt about it, wrote about it, envisioned it, took action when necessary, all of which I am about to share with you in this book - which by the way is another one of my dreams coming true!

I hope you enjoy reading this book and that it leads to you creating and living your very own dream life.

With love and light

Tanya Bardo

Chapter 1

You Are What You Think

You Are What You Think

I first read about the power of positive thinking when I was on maternity leave with my first born Gabriella and the thought of returning to the call centre to work 12 hour shifts for little more than minimum wage was filling me with dread.

I remember the book I was reading about positive thinking all those years ago started by saying what you are about to read will change your life and my goodness it changed my life alright! The book promised to make my dreams come true and it bloody did! The only thing I can't understand about positive thinking is why the hell does it not get taught to everybody as soon as they are old enough to understand? Once I finished reading the book I actually said out loud, 'Oh my God, this might actually be why my life has been so crappy lately!' I had attracted it with my negative thinking!

I became obsessed with everything to do with self-help and I even started to study the difference between a happy, successful person's behaviour and mindset compared to an unhappy unsuccessful person's behaviour and mindset. What became very clear was that it all boils down to one thing which is:

YOU ARE WHAT YOU THINK

Look around you. Look at your sofa, your TV, your bed, your house/flat, your shoes, your clothes. Look at every little thing. What do they all have in common? They all started as a thought in someone's mind.

Look at every couple you see. Even they started as a thought in someone's mind. For example, 'Wow, she's gorgeous, I am going to ask her out!'

Every argument you have or see or hear also started in someone's mind, maybe even yours.

Bad Thought

'Oh my God, he is so selfish, why can't he look after the kids for once, why is everything always left for me to do?'

Then these bad thoughts turn to feelings. You are thinking angry, negative thoughts, so you feel angry, then your feelings turn to actions.

Bad Action

Your partner walks through the door and you give him a piece of your mind! The selfish git! Which then leaves you with a bad reality.

Bad Reality

So now you and your partner are not talking because you had a go at him! He's gone out in a mood and you're left doing the stuff that your partner would have been doing if he was there. Great! And all of this started by one little negative thought in your mind that you choose to listen too. Every thought that comes in your head is just a thought. Just because it came into your head doesn't make it true, so you have the choice with every thought, whether to listen to it or dismiss it. If you had chosen to dismiss the thought and to think of something positive about your partner instead, then you would have ended up with a much better reality;

Bad Thought to Good Thought
"Oh my God he's so selfish blah blah blah...' But then recognise the negative thought as just a negative

thought and think of something more positive instead, for example, "He's not that bad really, he has had a busy past two weeks at work and probably deserves a break. After all, I love him and he loves me so much, so when he comes in I'll give him a hug and tell him I love him and then later on when we are having dinner I will explain in a nice way that I need a bit more help with the kids.

Good Action

Big kiss and hug with the man you love. Then you explain later in a calmer more positive way you would like more help and he replies, 'Of course darling.'

Good Reality

You have a lovely evening with the man you love.

Negative thoughts = negative feelings = negative actions = negative reality!
Positive thoughts = positive feelings = positive actions = positive reality.

Your life up until now has all been down to your thoughts and beliefs, which shape your actions, which shape your reality.

What we are thinking about determines whether our emotions are positive or negative. This is how I see it. When you are thinking negative thoughts like anger, jealousy, fear, worry, doubt etc., these thoughts make you feel bad and when you feel bad your energy is bad so you become a big bundle of negative energy, which makes you have negative actions, which attract negative things, people, circumstances to you like a magnet! This gives you a bad reality.

However when you think positive thoughts that make you feel happy or excited or joyful or loving or appreciative etc, you become a big happy beautiful whirlwind, sucking in and attracting all positive things, people and circumstances like a very powerful magnetic whirlwind! All the thoughts and images that are going on in your mind are what you are attracting to you.

If you are thinking good, you are attracting good, if you are thinking bad then you are attracting bad. So this is where I'd been going wrong! I'd been thinking about what I didn't want. I'd been thinking about my lack of money. I had been thinking about my job I hated. I had been thinking about my relationship that had gone down the pan and all these thoughts were making me feel bad, so I was just a big bundle of negative energy attracting more of the same. I realised very quickly that I had to change the thoughts and images in my mind if I wanted to change my life, because now I understood that if I am thinking negative thoughts which make me feel bad then I am going to continue getting a bad reality. I had to change my thoughts to what I wanted instead of what I didn't want so I wrote down on a piece of paper the things that were in my life at the moment that I didn't want which was a job I dreaded and having no money and being single. Then I thought actually being single could be quite fun if I had my dream job and money to provide a luxury life for my baby daughter, so I decided I would concentrate on getting my dream job, which for me was to be a model and I wrote in my little jotter how I would like my new life to be. It went something like this:

My name is Tanya Robinson. I am a successful, well-known model. I travel the world modelling, visiting beautiful places, enjoy all of my photo shoots and meet new friends and fascinating people. I am able to support me and by daughter by doing a job I love.

As I was writing how I would like my life to be I was imagining it in my mind (as everything you see in this world started in someone's imagination), seeing myself on photo shoots looking amazing, on airplanes travelling the world to my shoots and imaging myself shopping, buying all the things I had ever wanted. After half an hour of doing this I was buzzing! I was so excited just thinking about my new life and because I felt good I was attracting lots of other good things as well, I walked into a newsagents and there was a full stand of FHM magazines. FHM at the time was the most famous bestselling men's magazine in the world and on the front cover this month looking amazing was Carmen Electra. I wanted to be a cover girl just like her. I bought the magazine and took it home, studying all the pictures and imagined that I was Carmen, I was excited about my new life as a model. I was very aware that what I was thinking about was going to happen as everything you see started as a thought in somebody's mind, even the negative things you see. I made sure that I would try really hard to only think positive thoughts that made me happy so that I would attract good things and I would daydream imagining myself as a model living my dream life.

Obviously, as soon as you think about what you want,

it doesn't appear immediately. It takes a little bit of time, but don't let this put you off because trust me, it will appear as long as you keep imagining what you want and feel the feelings as if it is here with no doubt getting in the way. Sometimes it was hard at first to stay positive. Even though I was excited every time I thought of my new life, I would feel deflated waiting for it to happen, especially when I was working a 12 hour shift in the call centre and there were 320 calls waiting to be answered. But I knew that if I got down about it I would end up a big bundle of negative energy, making my actions negative and would never be able to attract my new positive life, so I looked for the positive in everything and everyone. Instead of moaning about my 12 hour shifts I would be grateful that I even had a job and that I was healthy enough to work and that all my co-workers were lovely and we had a laugh when there were no calls to take. With my new positive attitude I even started to enjoy taking the calls. I was even enjoying speaking to the grumpy customers and helping them so that they ended the call happy. I was loving life just by deciding to look for the good in everything and everyone. After a month of my new positive attitude I was reading the News of the World and there was a big advert saying that FHM magazine were looking for the first non-celebrity to grace the cover of their magazine and the winner would receive £10,000 and a modelling contact with a top modelling agency. As soon as I read it I thought this is the way in to my dream job that I had spent months dreaming about!

I sent my pictures off to FHM as soon as I got them developed from my little throw away camera from

Boots and waited excitedly. After a month of waiting and many phone calls from FHM magazine later, they called to say I had made it into the top 10! This was amazing, because they had had 6,000 entries. I would be flown to Gran Canaria for a photo shoot with the other 9 girls and our pictures would appear in the magazine for the readers to vote for the winner. We would also film a reality TV show for the viewers to vote as well. I couldn't believe it! I was over the moon! I was skipping around like happy feet!

I was flown to Gran Canaria to a beautiful 5 star hotel and met with all the lovely FHM team and the other girls who had successfully made the top 10. Everybody was very excited but it didn't take long before some of the 9 girls were bitching about each other and moaning about this and that and they didn't like their hair or make up or styling for their photo shoot. I on the other hand was the opposite. I was so excited and grateful to be there I gave thanks for everything and enjoyed every single second of the experience. I returned home on a high and couldn't wait for the pictures to appear in FHM and the T.V show to be aired.

The day FHM was due out I got up at 8am and got in my car and drove straight to the shop and bought the magazine. It had the beautiful Halle Berry on the cover and I couldn't wait till I got home. I opened it up and there I was a big double page spread all to myself and I looked gorgeous! I was so happy! The other 9 girls only had a single page each and some of the girls shared a single page with another girl. Well serves you right for being negative Nellies I thought... Then my dad rang to say I was in most of the newspapers and again I had the bigger picture than all the other contestants, I was ecstatic I was also picked by FHM's PR company to be interviewed on all the main morning TV shows and radio stations. It was all incredibly exciting. Four weeks later a one hour special of the follow-up to the reality TV show where FHM would reveal the winner of the first ever FHM High Street Honeys competition.

The day had arrived and I felt physically sick with nerves but at the same time so excited, I had my mum and dad and sister Sherrie there, which made the day even more special. I sat with the other 9 contestants in a line while the presenter Andy Goldstein read out third-place... It wasn't me. I could hear my heart beating, it was so loud, I was so close to my dream I could touch it. Then he read out second place. Again, it wasn't me. Then for what seemed like forever... AND THE WINNNNNNNER ISSSSSSSSS...........TANYA ROBINSON!

Oh my God! Oh my God! Oh my God! I had won! I can't even explain the happiness I felt, I was over the moon! I was whisked off to a 5 star hotel for pictures and interviews for the next day's papers, then had an early night because I had a 3 day photo shoot ahead of me where I would be the first ever non-celebrity to grace the cover of FHM! Wow! This is the weird part. I did 5 front covers for FHM in my modelling career and one was a replica of the Carmen Electra cover that I had studied all that time ago! You really do end up with what you think about! I had £10,000 in my bank account the day I won, I was in every newspaper, on all the morning TV shows, local news , local papers. Every time I walked into a shop there were shelves of magazines with ME on the cover of them! It was unbelievable. I even had a pub change its name to Tanya's Charms in my honour. FHM sent me a massive bottle of champagne and bunch of beautiful flowers with a card thanking me for my hard work and to let me know that my front cover had outsold their biggest ever selling Jennifer Lopez cover! A single mum from Yorkshire who worked in a call centre had outsold Jennifer Lopez! Wow! Then I had a phone call from my agent who FHM had set me up with. I would fly to Jamaica for a photo shoot with News of the World for 7 days, then I would fly to Miami for a photo shoot!

Everything I had been thinking about and imagining

had come true in some shape or form. I had gone from a skint single mum with a job I didn't like to a well-known model travelling the world with a full bank account! I was so excited and grateful and happy, which of course was making me a big happy beautiful whirlwind sucking in and attracting all positive things, people, and circumstances like a very powerful magnet. My agent called me and said there is a casting for the new Lynx advert tomorrow and would like me to go. I had no experience of things like that, I never took drama at school. Just go, said my agent, you get experience while doing it! Yes, she was right. I was filled with excitement. I loved all the Lynx adverts, I would love to be in one! I started imagining myself getting the job, feeling so excited! I arrived at the casting and there were corridors and corridors full of what seemed like every model in the country! And they were all beautiful, stunning and much taller than me, which isn't hard as I am only 5'3". A few doubts popped in my head like Arrrrgggghhhhh, these girls are amazing catwalk models who have probably got loads of experience and I am just a shortish single mum from Yorkshire who only has experience in a call centre. I quickly rubbished those thoughts and congratulated myself that I was even there because 80% of success is showing up! I got excited again. There were so many girls there. We were obviously waiting a long time, much to the annoyance to a lot of the moaning models, but I was just grateful that I was even in the queue for a Lynx advert. The casting went really well and I went home happy and proud of myself for doing my best, then my agent called me screaming, 'You have got the Lynx advert job! They want you!' Arrrrggggghhhh, that's brilliant news! I filmed the Lynx advert and was paid 3 times more in one day by Lynx than I earned working 12 hour shifts for a whole year! I was invited to all the celebrity parties. I could write a book on everything that happened to me but I will stick with writing this book instead of boring you with juicy gossip, hehe... This positive thinking really works!

Chapter 2

Don't Get Bitter. Get BETTER!

Don't Get Bitter. Get BETTER!

Unfortunately, sometimes in life, things go wrong. Sometimes everything is wonderful but sometimes shit happens. Sometimes devastating things happen, like somebody you love dearly dies, or you get divorced from someone you thought was your soul mate, or you lose your house and all your belongings. There is a never-ending stream of shit that can happen on this glorious life journey.

The problem is, you have no control over most of what happens in life, but what you do have is the control over how you deal with what life throws at you.

People always say that time heals but that is simply because it takes people a long time to change their mindset. So it is not actually the time, which has healed you; your change in mindset is the true healer.

Life can seem to be going great you're on cruise control, then all of a sudden BAM! Out of nowhere life throws you a devastating blow. Well you have two choices. You can either sit and wallow in a state of denial, crying and asking 'Why me?' or you can accept it's happened and you can't change it and get on with it. You are a very strong person who can bounce back. You may be thinking 'But you don't know what's happened to me! There is no way on earth I can come back from this!' Maybe you are thinking I am being very harsh and a bit heartless. Yes, you may be a victim, but as long as you act like one you will remain one which is no fun for you or all the people around you. No matter what happens in life, life always goes on and you don't want to be left behind. So come on, chin up, love, and read on.

I recently lost my amazing, special grandad. We had a very strong bond. I watched him take his last breath as he lost his long, painful battle with cancer. There are no words to describe the pain I felt as I watched him leave me, I was heartbroken and when I say heartbroken I mean my heart was broken. I was in physical pain in my heart, like it had been ripped apart and stamped on over and over and over again. I was distraught. Why, my grandad? Why, why, why? I need him, I love him. He was only 72 years old. Give me him back! Please! but after a week of non-stop crying, I envisioned my grandad saying to me, 'Come on, love, you'll see me again soon enough. Start living before you join me up here.'

I miss my grandad every day and even more so at family get togethers, I have my wedding coming up and I am devastated that he won't be there, so I'm having a big canvas picture of him in the church and above the top table and I know he will be looking down on me smiling.

Life is very short, so even though the tears still come, I don't wallow as much I did before. I know that I will be up there joining him before I know it, so I need to make every day count and live a little bit extra for him in the time I have left here.

I would like to make clear though, if you feel upset, don't suppress your feelings. When you cry, excess stress chemicals are pushed out of your body, stabalising the body's balance. That's why you feel lighter after you've had a good cry. Crying is nature's way of relieving anxiety. You always feel better after a good cry. Don't suppress it and hold it in, let those tears roll! Get it all out feel lighter and get better. Cry out the bitterness, then get better.

"The past cannot be changed, the future is yet in your power." Mary Pickford

Sometimes it's hard to reject that bitterness away. Holding onto anger and bitterness only hurts you, not the person who has done you wrong. I'm going to tell you my poor me sob story of this year. (P.S. I don't mind if you get bored and move to the next chapter, but try and stick with it, ok?)

I gave birth to my third child on 7th March 2013, a beautiful, perfect baby boy called Renz Tommy (Tommy after my grandad who I had recently lost) Robinson-Bardsley.

About 10 days after I gave birth I couldn't stop crying, I had the baby blues which most mothers get. But in this instance it didn't go away and everything carried on looking bleak. It became apparent that I had post-natal depression. I recognised the signs straight away as I suffered from post-natal depression with my first born, Gabriella. Depression is the worst feeling in the world and if left untreated can spiral out of control and get even worse. So it's important not to just think that it will go away or that you can handle it on your own, go to the doctor who can help you. Don't be afraid of taking medication, depression is so common and very treatable and can be controlled easily with the right help, so don't struggle on your own.

A little while after giving birth we had a big family party for my brother-in-laws 18th in Manchester, which would be my first night out since having Renz . I got all dressed up in a new dress with two pairs of spanx to hide the remaining jelly belly. I had a great night with friends and family, lots of laughing, dancing and drinking. We celebrated with champagne and as it was my first night out in a long while, it didn't take much to get me more than a little bit tipsy. Phil and I were staying at a top Hotel in Manchester. In the very early hours of the morning I returned to the hotel room and took off my dress and spanx and face-planted the bed into a deep, deep drunken sleep. Phil left the hotel room to go on a lads' day out, leaving me there in a drunken, comatosed sleep. I woke up in a hazy state to find a strange man at the side of my bed touching me. I screamed for him to get out. I then rang Phil who quickly came with a car full of his friends and he rang the police. I was badly shaken up. Phil asked me why I'd put the Do Not Disturb sign on the door. This sent me cold as I hadn't, the man must have done this. The police came and were brilliant. They closed the room off for forensics and explained because I was out of it with all the alcohol I had drunk, they needed to send me to St Mary's hospital to be fully checked out to make sure he hadn't done anything else to me. I had external and internal swabs which in itself was distressing. Luckily for me the tests came back that I hadn't been raped, just sexually assaulted. Thoughts kept going around and around in my head, how many other drunken girls might have been targeted?

Within 24 hours the police arrested a male member of staff at the hotel. A few weeks later I found out from the police that a female cleaner had come into my room twice but couldn't wake me to ask if I wanted the room cleaning. She had seen that I was on the bed naked and wouldn't wake up, so when she saw the mini bar guy in the corridor she told him not to go into my room as there was a sleeping naked girl in there. He chose to ignore this information and came into my room. He was a clever guy, he covered his back as to why his DNA should be on me or my bedsheets. He said he came in to change the mini bar (after he was told to stay out of my room by the cleaner) and said he noticed I was fast asleep and naked with my arm hanging off the edge of the bed. He said he was worried that I would get cold, so he came over, lifted me onto the bed and covered me up. He denied putting the Do Not Disturb sign on the door, even though neither Phil, me or the cleaner had put it there.

Months went by, waiting for the police to get forensics back and for the case to go to the Crown Prosecution Service to decide if there was enough evidence to go to court. After 5 months of it hanging over my head, the CPS came back and said that they felt there wasn't enough evidence. I went cold, I was so angry and disgusted that this man would get away scot free. He had admitted to the police about coming into my room twice while I was naked and out cold, and he had admitted to coming over and moving my naked sleeping body. The police had the statement of the cleaner who had told the man I was in the room naked and wasn't responding and not to go in there. Yet he still came into my room twice! But the CPS still didn't think there was enough evidence to take it to court. I felt physically sick!

I have since found out that 95% of rape cases don't even bother reporting it to the police as they don't believe in the justice system and that of the 5% who build up the courage to tell the police, only 40% make it to court as it's his word against her word.

At first I was angry and bitter that he had got away with it. I had to keep reminding myself that my being angry was only harming me and those people close to me, not him. So I just had to let it go. For the first couple of months after the incident I wouldn't stay in a hotel but I soon forced myself to do it. I love traveling the world and I am not going to let one man take that away from me.

I was so lucky that I had Phil through those horrible days. He was my rock and didn't leave my side.

Two months after it happened I woke up on the morning of my birthday and the incident was front page news. I then started getting abuse on Twitter from internet trolls about Phil and I. I don't care what people say about me, as the saying goes, it's none of my business what other people think of me. But when they slag my family off it hurts a lot more as I'm very protective of my family, especially Phil and my babies.

Bullies, especially the cowards who bully on the internet at home feeling all brave behind a computer, are weak insecure cowards who are normal eaten up inside with jealousy. They are called internet trolls for a reason and the reason is that they resemble trolls, ugly inside. Don't let their ugly words get to you, don't waste your precious time thinking about what they have said and certainly never believe it to be true.

Unfortunately we now live in a world where success brings internet trolls, don't let this stop you. It just means you're doing something right.

Bullies, especially internet bullies, are normally victims and something negative has happened to them in the past but they have chosen to get bitter instead of getting better. All you can do is ignore and block them and mentally send the negative individuals love and wish them better - and report them of course.

"If you can't say anything nice, don't say anything at all."

Bambi - Thumper's mum to Thumper

After my post natal depression, sexual assault and Twitter abuse, my house was robbed and was absolutely trashed in a search for cash. Even though it was devastating, I had two choices, as everyone does when shit happens – get bitter or get better. I sure as hell didn't want to turn into one of those ugly horrible trolls, so I decided to get better. No matter what happens in life a smile and a just get on with it attitude will always pull you through.

So after reading my latest sob story, how did you feel? Bored? Unless you're speaking to a therapist most people eventually get a little bit tired and bored of listening to sob stories after a while. Obviously give yourself a little time to let the tears roll, but don't drag it out. Everyone has their fair share of misfortune there is always someone in the world worse off than you, so you don't want to be one of those negative individuals who everyone wants to avoid. So come on, get better!

"Smile and the world smiles with you, cry and you cry alone."
Stanley Gordon West

So after any shit that life throws at you, you have two choices:

Get bitter

or

Get better

Should you ever find yourself victim of other people's bitterness, smallness or insecurities, just remember it's their issue not yours so don't get caught up in their drama, you are far too busy being fabulous.

Hopefully you have chosen to get better because after all, everyone knows that the best revenge is success, so read to see how to get better, create and start living your dream life, get your dream job, your dream body. Build your confidence and self-esteem as high as they will go, look the best you ever have. Unlock your true potential and be the best that you can be. Negative thoughts like anger, jealousy and bitterness only hurt you, they don't hurt those you are angry with. So the only thing to do is to forgive and let it go. Always forgive but that doesn't always mean you have to let them back into your life. You can forgive and move on. You're not a door mat, you're strong and amazingly fabulous.

So now we have decided that no matter what happens or who is to blame, you are not going to get bitter, you are going to let it go and get better. So let's start getting better... a lot better! Everyone can lead their dream life no matter what has happened in the past, especially you, so let's go.

Chapter 3

'Worry is a Misuse of Imagination'

Dan Zadra

'Worry is a Misuse of Imagination' Dan Zadra

All Negative Thoughts are Mind Bullshit

All negative thoughts are mind bullshit. The good news is you don't have to put up with it any longer. If you let your mind do what it wants it will run around making up all sorts of negative paranoid bullshit, which can be very damaging to you, your health, your relationships, and your work etc. Take control of your mind and only take notice of positive thoughts. Now we are only human so we are always going to have a few negative thoughts, AKA mind bullshit that enters our head. But what we need to do is dismiss it as soon as possible. Recognise it's just mind bullshit and that just because it's popped in your head doesn't mean it's true or you have to investigate it. Just dismiss it and think positive thoughts of things that make you happy.

You will know if you are thinking happy positive thoughts because you will be feeling good. But if you're listening and wallowing in mind bullshit you will know because you will feel like shit! It's really quite simple. If you think, "My God, I feel like shit," then realise it's because you're thinking negative thoughts AKA wallowing in mind bullshit. As soon as you realise, quickly change your thoughts to happy positive ones.

Sometimes I can't think of anything positive to think about when I'm feeling shit so what I've learnt to do is think, "What negative thought was I thinking a few minutes ago that has caused me to feel this shit?" You might have been thinking. "Oh yes I was thinking about the fact that my boyfriend cheated on me and on top of that I've got a shit car!" Well, thoughts like that are obviously going to make you feel like you feel nothing but shit and attract it into your life. Change them to the opposite. Start thinking about how you've just got engaged to a gorgeous guy, he's perfect and a million times better than your ex who cheated on you in every way. He has also bought you a fabulous new sports car just because he loves you. It's on your drive with a big red bow on it. All the neighbours gather round to look at your amazing new car and guy and your ex just happens to be walking down your street at that very moment to see it all... Now doesn't this feel much better? Don't then become deflated because it's not true, because remember - that what you're thinking and feeling becomes your reality. If you continue your thinking about the stuff that makes you feel bad, the mind bullshit, then you're only going to get more of the same – a bad reality. If you're thinking about what you are going to get then it makes serious sense to think about what you would like and what would make you happy. Thinking negative thoughts makes us feel like shit and will only bring shit into our lives, it makes no sense to WORRY.

Worry is nothing more than a load of mind bullshit! It's been proven that only about 5% of worry ever comes true, so that's 95% of wasted time on bullshit, that makes you feel shit, when you could have been out in the world being happy. If the thought doesn't make you feel good, it's mind bullshit. All you need to do is recognise it...

I'm fat and ugly and always will be... BULLSHIT.

I'm stupid... BULLSHIT!

I can't get a man... BULLSHIT!

Now once you've recognised your mind bullshit, all you need to do is smile and change it to how you want it to be. Change it to what would make you happy....

I have a gorgeous sexy body.

I am clever and smart.

I have men begging me for dates.

But these new beliefs about me having a gorgeous sexy body and being clever and smart and men begging me for dates are bullshit I hear you cry! Well you chose to believe all that negative bullshit so why not replace it with positive bullshit? If you choose to listen and believe your mind bullshit then trust me, you will attract bullshit and your life will be bullshit.

What you think about all day long becomes your reality, so it makes sense to only think positive things about yourself and your life, that is what you will attract. We bring experiences that fulfil our expectations and beliefs. Expect and believe only good things and you will attract only good things. Your reality will be the life of your dreams.

'My life has been full of terrible misfortunes, most of which have never happened.'
Michel De Montaigne

When I first learned about positive thinking I still had negative thoughts, "Arrrrgggggghhhhhh! Noooooo! I'm going attract bad things! Arrrrggghhhhhh!" I would worry about every bad thought I had, bringing more negative thoughts. But please don't worry because we are only human. It's only natural that we will sometimes have negative bad moods and sometimes it's healthy to cry and scream. What's not healthy is dwelling on it for any longer than needs be. And what's good to know is a positive thought is a stronger magnet than a negative thought. So if you want to be in a bad mood every now and again, just go ahead! Once I started allowing myself to be in a bad mood if I wanted, then I rarely was because I was allowed. Just like now I let myself have hot chocolate fudge cake whenever I want, so I never do because I'm allowed!

We always want what we can't have, so never deny yourself anything, especially a bad mood!

Chapter 4

How Do You See Yourself?

How Do You See Yourself?

The way you see yourself can be one of the biggest obstacles holding you back from living your dream life and being the best you can be. I would like you to complete the following exercise to remove any negative obstacles that might be standing in your way

Exercise

List the things you do not like about yourself and your life. This can be anything to do with your life, your looks, your personality, your love life, or your work life/job.

- ⚹ I'm shy
- ⚹ I'm short tempered with everybody
- ⚹ I'm fat and ugly
- ⚹ I'm unlucky in love

Your list can be as long or as short as you wish. Now you have your completed list I want you to list why you think these things that you do not like are true. What/who made you believe these things to be true?

For example

I am shy.

My mum and dad always tell people I'm shy. I always have been and I feel and act shy.

I'm short tempered with everybody.

Everybody says I've got a temper on me and I always fall out with people because of it, especially my family.

I'm fat and ugly.
I've always been fat and ugly. I got bullied for being fat and ugly when I was at school and I never get chatted up by men. When I look in the mirror I can see that I'm fat and ugly.

I'm unlucky in love.
I've been single for over two years. I've had a few flings but all the men in my life have broken my heart or been complete losers.

OK, so now you have your list of things you do not like about yourself and your life. Now just because you believed these things to be true in the past and you saw/heard evidence for these things to be true in the past, does it make it true today?

Do you want these things to be true today?

Look at your limiting beliefs one at a time and ask yourself: Is that actually true, what proof do I have that my belief is 100% factually true?

(And because you know it is or a nasty cow said it to you in an argument is not proof!)

Let's get one thing straight:

You are good enough just the way you are!

You have the power to be whoever you want to be. Just because you thought of yourself or believed yourself to be shy or bad tempered or ugly or fat in the past it doesn't mean you have to be today. Today is a new day and it's time to stop letting old, limiting beliefs about yourself and your life stop you from going, getting and living your dream life.

Now I want you to finish this exercise by rewriting your beliefs how you want them to be.

I used to be shy... but now... I'm confident in every situation.

I used to be bad tempered... but now... I'm patient and easy going. I just laugh at things that used to get me angry.

I used to be fat and ugly.... but now... I'm looking and

feeling good. I love what I see when I look in the mirror.

I used to be unlucky in love... but now... I'm very lucky in love.

In doing this you have now created your new positive beliefs. I want you to write them down somewhere where you can have easy access to them. Stick them up on your bedroom wall or write them in a little notepad and have it next to your bed. I want you to read them every morning when you wake up and every night before you go to sleep.

- ⋏ I'm confident in every situation.
- ⋏ I'm patient and easy going and I laugh at the things that used to make me angry.

- A I'm looking and feeling good. I love what I see when I look in the mirror.
- A I'm very lucky in love.

Now you have your new beliefs on paper, I want you to bring them to life. I want you to act as if they are true. Just pretend they are true if you don't believe it to begin with because when you pretend and act as if you're confident, patient, happy, etc. then you will start to see evidence of your new positive beliefs. Eventually, they will become your new beliefs and then your beliefs become your reality.

Now that you have your new beliefs you need to keep repeating them in your head or out loud as often as possible. At the very least always first thing in the morning and last thing before you go to sleep at night.

This is when your mind is at its most receptive, making your new beliefs sink into your subconscious. I normally find changing beliefs takes about 3 weeks of thinking about them morning and night, but if you can add the action to go with the thought, all the better.

For example, say your new belief is "I am confident" and you not only think it but pretend you are confident in all situations even if you don't feel it, you will soon become it.

"Fake it until you make it!"

It will be well worth the effort, the results will be positively life-changing. You may find that as you are repeating your life-changing beliefs you have those pesky little negative thoughts telling you that this is never going to work and it's pointless. Ignore them.

The sky is absolutely NOT the limit, there's a whole universe out there!

Chapter 5

What Do You Want?

What Do You Want?

So to recap, changing your belief system is similar to growing a beautiful plant.

1. Take the time to buy the right seeds (Choose your thoughts and beliefs)

2. Plant the seeds (Say your new positive beliefs)

3. Pull out any weeds (Tell the negative thoughts to back off)

4. Water the plants (Repeat and affirm your new positive thoughts and beliefs)

5. Watch your beautiful plant grow and flourish (Watch your confidence grow and your life turn into your dream life)

What Do You Want?

What do you want? It sounds a simple question but through my experience coaching it's the one question my clients have the hardest time answering.

This is because over the years we have been conditioned by well-meaning parents, guardians, aunties, uncles, grandparents, teachers, friends etc that life is not a fairy tale and you can't always have what we want, so you might as well forget about that wild dream or you will just end up disappointed. I remember saying to my mum and dad when I was about 9 years old that I wanted to be a model when I grew up and my dad replied, "Well you need to think of something else you want to do as well, Tanya, because there are millions of pretty girls out there." I remember feeling deflated, thinking my dream was unobtainable. My dad wasn't being mean saying that;

he was trying to protect me. He was just doing to me what had been done to him. He was preparing me for the attitude that most people have - life's not easy and I might be left disappointed. I'm sure if I hadn't learned about positive thoughts and their effect I would have taught the same to my children. But life is easy and you can be and achieve anything you want when you know how. I have since managed to teach my dad the power of positive thinking, he told me he had been visualising getting a jaguar car and guess what's arriving in two weeks? A brand New Jaguar! See you can teach old dogs new tricks, he'll kill me when he reads this.

So back to the question, what do you want? I'm not asking- what do you think you can realistically have? I am asking if you had a magic wand what would you want in your life?

Here are some questions which will help you imagine your ideal future. I want you to answer the questions in present tense as if it is already true; because if you write 'I want to spend my days...' then you will always be left wanting, so make sure that doesn't happen. You need to write, 'I spend my days...'

Writing down your visions or dreams of how you would like your life to be as if it is true today is incredibly powerful. Every time I've written down my dreams, in a place where I can read them daily (for me it's in a special private notepad), I've watched all my dreams turn to reality before my eyes.

Also, when answering the questions I want you to write what you truly want your life to be like, not just what you think you can realistically have.

- How do you want to spend your days?
- How do you want to spend your evenings and nights?
- What is in this life that excites you?
- Who is living this life with you?
- Where do you live?
- What do you look like?
- What do you feel like?
- What challenges are you looking forward to?
- What will your contribution to others be in this life?

Now that you have answered these questions you have a good understanding of what you want. So go ahead and think about it and imagine it as if it's already happening to you, feeling the good excited feelings as if they are here now. You're living your dream life. The more you think about feeling good, the quicker you will magnetise it into your life.

The reason most people don't get what they want in life is because they spend most of their time thinking about, worrying about and imagining what they don't want, which brings them exactly what they didn't want. Control your thoughts and you will control your life. The thoughts and images you hold in your mind are what you are creating and bringing to life. If you don't want it, don't think about it, push away any thought of what you don't want. Think about what you do want instead and you will get that instead of what you don't want.

Now you know what you want, let's go get it!

"A lot of people are afraid to say what they want, that's why they don't get what they want."
Madonna

Paint on Your New Canvas

Now you have got rid of all those negative beliefs that have been holding you back, you are a blank canvas. Start painting on your new positive beliefs. There are a number of ways to do this, so you can choose which way is best for you. I personally use and practise them all. The first way is so simple yet so effective; I call it my 'Dreams to Reality' book.

Dreams to Reality Book

A 'Dreams to Reality' book can be any jotter or

notepad (I would buy a thick one that is small enough to travel with so you can keep it with you at all times) or you can buy a Dreams to Reality book from Tanyabardo.com. Once you have your 'Dreams to Reality' book and a pen at the ready I want you to start by listing everything you are grateful for; everything from your family and friends to your house with heating and running water. Be thankful for your eyesight, your beautiful face, your boyfriend/husband or your exciting single life; just anything and everything.

Then I want you to list every compliment you have ever received from anybody, from your parents to a builder shouting 'You're gorgeous!' in the street.
Then list all your new beliefs that replace the old ones that were holding you back. For example, I wrote in

my 'Dreams to Reality' book 'I am lucky in love.' I wrote this in my notepad when I was very unlucky in love. I was a single mum but after changing my beliefs and writing it in my notepad, reading it and affirming it every day, it became my new belief, which became my reality.

I also want you to write down all your ideas and inspirations. Some of these might come when you're in the shower, just about to go to sleep or while you're driving. Keep your book and a pen close to you so you can add them because they are important and they could be the start of something amazing. Everything stems from your thoughts. Look around you now, your sofa, your TV, your bed, your house/flat, your clothes, your shoes. Look at every little thing around you. What do they all have in common? They all started as a thought in someone's mind. If you have a good idea that excites you then don't just dismiss it, write it in your 'Dreams to Reality' book, as if it was true today, and watch the people and circumstances you need come into your life to make it happen. This book you are reading now started as a little thought in my mind that excited me.

Write any positive quotes that make you feel good.

Write down all of your dreams for the future as if they are true today. Sometimes when I doubt that I can achieve a new dream, I re-read my old dreams out of my 'Dreams to Reality' book that became my reality.

I've said this before but I can't put into words how powerful writing your dreams down is! Remember to write them as if they are true today. Try it and watch miracles happen.

Read and affirm everything in your 'Dreams to Reality' book at least once a day. I read mine every morning when I wake up to get me vibrating good energy for the day ahead. It makes me feel happy and positive as well as increasing my confidence and wellbeing.

Vision Boards

Another great way to get you excited about and attracting your dreams is by creating a vision board. Creating your vision board is fun to do and it really works. Cut out pictures of all the things you wish to attract into your life and put them on your vision board. You can put absolutely anything you want on there, your dream home, your dream car etc. When I was a single mum and there was just me and my daughter Gabriella, I cut out a man from a catalogue and put a question mark on the man's head, trusting that the universe would bring me the perfect partner. I also cut out a baby boy and stuck us all together on my vision board. Now this has become my reality because I met Phil and we had a perfect baby boy together. Gabriella and I love them both very much. I also got the Audi, Bentley and the dream home I put on my vision board. I then wanted another baby to add to our happy family so I put another baby on my vision board and a year later our beautiful baby Renz was born. It's spooky but vision boards really do work; they are amazing. It's also a good way to keep focused on what it is you want to be magnetising into your life. Go have fun and create your reality.

If struggling, refer back to the questions in Chapter 5 about how you spend your days, your evenings, Where would you live? Who'd be there with you? Gather up pictures of all these things, this will help to bring your dreams alive visually.

Your 'Dreams to Reality' and your vision board are amazing at turning your dreams into reality because the thoughts and images that are in your mind the most, are what you are bringing to you and will in time become your reality. They are good at motivating you into taking action.

Be aware of social media as the words and images you look at all day will appear as your own reality. I read an article the other day about a girl who loved reading internet trolls comments, I was horrified for her as I knew she was only attracting misery into her own life. I only follow positive people on social media sites and I always try my best to only upload positive posts, your social networks act as your very own vision boards without you even realising it.

Chapter 6

Preparation is the Key to Success

Preparation is the Key to Success

"One important key to success is self-confidence. An important key to self-confidence is preparation."
Arthur Ashe

An athlete can't expect to turn up to a race at the Olympics with no practice or training and expect to win. I can't expect to turn up to a big night out and feel gorgeous without putting thought an effort into my hair and outfit. Likewise I can't expect to be strong, fit, healthy and look hot if I don't take the time and effort to workout. You can't expect any work meeting to go well without working on and preparing the material beforehand. You can't expect a talk in front of a lot of people to go well if you haven't practiced what you are going to say.

You can't expect to perform a perfect song without learning the words, practicing, warming up your vocal chords.

"The past cannot be changed, the future is yet in your power."
Mary Pickford

"A goal without a plan is just a wish."
Antoine de St-Exupery

If you have chosen to take the road to the better you, the best you can possibly be, then you need to prepare. Firstly you need to prepare your mind for success, you cannot find or reach success if your mind is still in negative or bitterness mode. So out with the negative and in with new positive thoughts.

Your life until now has all been down to your thoughts and beliefs which shaped your actions which shaped your reality.

For you to achieve your successful new dream, you have to be extremely high in confidence. You gain confidence by being successful but how do you get the confidence to go get the first success to kick start your confidence?

CHANGE YOUR THOUGHTS AND BELIEFS

CHANGE THE WAY YOU TALK TO YOURSELF

You need to train your mind with the thoughts and beliefs you want to be your reality. You have to take control of your mind and be disciplined with it because if you let your mind have a free rein you could be in for a depressing old bumpy ride.

Our thoughts and beliefs shape our life. You will be amazed at how many of your beliefs are so outdated and are holding you back from your dream life.

In sport you can do all the physical training you like, but if you don't keep it up then your physical training will go to waste. Just as your body needs constant exercise to be in top form, so does your mind.

This is the biggest most powerful reason why people's confidence goes up and down. It's their mind talk – your mind talk is how you speak to yourself in your head. That little voice in your head can make you strong or weak. If you just let your mind talk do whatever it wants, it can end up taking you on a roller coaster of negative emotions, so it's time to take control of it to get the results you want!

The only thing that stops you being confident and the best you can be is your limiting negative thoughts.

If a negative thought pops in your head, dismiss it and replace it with a positive affirmation even if you don't believe your new positive thought just yet. For example, "I am the best," or "I am ready," or "I am the best in my field." If you keep chanting them or saying them in your head, you will eventually believe them. When you do begin to believe them your feelings change, your actions change and your reality will be amazing!

It is perfectly normal for negative thoughts to keep coming back into your head but keep ignoring them and replacing them with positive thoughts and they will become less frequent.

You can't get your confidence from any outside sources, you have to get it from within and it starts by changing your mind talk. You don't need anyone's praise or compliments to make you feel good, you can do this for yourself.

Preparation + Opportunity = LUCK

Seneca

Think, Imagine, Believe

Think about and imagine what you want is here and believe you can have it with no doubt or feelings of unworthiness getting in the way. Remember you can have and be anything you want, everything is possible no matter what situation you are in at the moment, the power is in you!

FOR THE IMPOSSIBLE TO BECOME POSSIBLE YOU HAVE

TO BELIEVE THE IMPOSSIBLE IS POSSIBLE

It is very important to think about what you want because you're most dominant thought becomes your reality. Now if you have some old beliefs from your past, don't let them hold you back from thinking, imagining and believing that you can achieve your dreams. For example, here are some of the most common old beliefs I hear from my new clients why they can't achieve and live their dream lives,

- ⋏ I'm too old
- ⋏ I'm too fat
- ⋏ I'm not clever enough
- ⋏ I haven't got the right qualifications
- ⋏ I'm not pretty enough
- ⋏ The competition's too stiff, I can't compete
- ⋏ I'm too short (this one was the belief that stopped me from even attempting my dream as a top model. All that wasted time!)
- ⋏ I'm not good enough

These old beliefs are just the tip of the iceberg. You

might identify with some of them yourself and you may be able to add a lot more to the list. Thoughts like these are what actually go through people's heads and the beliefs are so strong that it actually stops them from going for, getting and living their dream lives. You know what? They are not true, they are just excuses that our mind has made up. It's all mind bullshit.

Belief is a powerful thing. From the age of 5 I always believed I was the best at every sport. This belief worried my mum because the day before sports day, when I was 5, I said, "Mummy, when I win all my races tomorrow, can I please send my prizes to Daddy?" (My dad was away on tour in Bosnia with the army.) My mum was worried I would be so upset and disappointed if I didn't win anything. So she tried to explain to me that you never know the outcome of things, even if you don't win it doesn't matter, it's the taking part that counts. I looked at her with no doubt in my mind and replied, "Mummy I will win!" And sure enough I won every single race I was in. This attitude with sport stayed with me until I was about 16. I started smoking, drinking, I grew boobs and discovered boys! So the sport went out the window but until then I was the captain of the netball, hockey and athletics teams. I only ever thought of winning. I only ever pictured myself winning. I only ever thought that there would be one outcome and that was me winning. I expected it and it came every time. Start believing, thinking and acting like a winner and life can only bring you a winning outcome.

Chapter 7

The Must Have Attitude For Success

The Must Have Attitude For Success

Stay Positive

It's very important to stay positive as;

POSITIVE THOUGHTS = POSITIVE FEELINGS = POSITIVE ENERGY = POSITIVE ACTIONS = POSITIVE REALITY!

The easiest way to stay positive is by focusing on all the good aspects of life. Get happy now, smile, read your Dreams to Reality every day, love and appreciate everyone and everything in your life and be grateful and inspired.

Get Happy Now

Always try to force yourself out of a crap negative

mood and into a happy beautiful positive whirlwind to attract all good things to you.

The fastest way to achieve your dreams is to enjoy the journey. The first thing we need to get straight is things, other people and money cannot make you happy. For instance I hear a lot of people say things like, "I'll be happy once I get a new car," or "I'll be happy when I find a new man," or "I'll be happy if I get the pay rise I want." Well, the only thing wrong with this is you will never get these things if you are not happy first. So you need to think, be and feel happy to attract a happy reality. If you depend on other people and things to make you happy then you are going to lead a very sad life, you have to find happiness within yourself first, then you will find that the people and the things you desired start to flow abundantly into your life. You are as happy as you decide to be! You have control over your mind, so you have a choice. You can either dwell on sad, negative thoughts that will only attract sad, negative thoughts, or you can choose to dismiss those negative thoughts and only think happy positive thoughts.

What makes us happy? Happy thoughts.

"There is nothing either good or bad, but thinking makes it so."
Shakespeare

Smile

Never underestimate just smiling. Smile at everyone and everything and watch the world become a beautiful friendly place. When you smile it makes you more attractive. When you smile it makes you appear more friendly, approachable and warmer. A smile cheers you up and those around_you. You can light up a room with a smile but most importantly when you smile it makes you feel good and when you_feel good you attract nothing but good into your life. Smiling gives you a natural high. It takes less muscles to smile than it does to frown. Even if you're feeling sad and fed up, just make your face smile, as this action tricks your brain to feel positive. It then releases mood-improving chemicals including natural painkillers.

Smiling boosts your immune system as your body is more relaxed. Smiling also makes you look younger by giving you a natural face lift. A smile literally pulls your face up from the sides and voilà, a younger happy face. So go on, give us a smile! :-)

Read Your Dreams to Reality Book Everyday

Start your day by reading your Dreams to Reality book the first opportunity you get in the morning whether that's before the kids wake up, whilst eating your breakfast or when travelling to work. Reminding yourself of all the things you have to be grateful for and all the compliments you have ever received. Now your new positive beliefs, dreams and ideas will get your day off to a good beginning, getting you in a good mood and feeling motivated and excited about the day ahead. So whatever you give your attention to, you also give your energy to, which will bring you everything you want much more quickly.

Love and Appreciate Everyone and Everything

If you're feeling down or irritated or just generally negative, look around you and start to appreciate everything and everyone and watch your bad mood melt away. So many people just plod through their days like it's a chore to get through them. They get their kids up ready for school, argue with their partner because they slept in, shout at the kids because they are misbehaving and all they want to do is get back in bed and ignore the world. I know this because I have lived those days. STOP! Open your eyes and be present, look at your children's beautiful faces and your partner's gorgeous face and just love and appreciate them. If this was your last day with them, would you be bothered that you all slept in and were running late or your children were messing about? No you would not. So appreciate them and give them love every chance you get. The same goes for all your family and friends and even work colleges, even the ones that get on your nerves!

Try to enjoy every day as if it was your last. Would you spend your last day on earth in your PJ's with a right arse on, feeling sorry for yourself? Didn't think so. Get up off your behind and do something productive or be with the people you love and appreciate them and love them. Even if they do get on your nerves sometimes, so what? Just love and appreciate them for who they are. Even when my dad is going round the house, switching all the lights off, moaning, "IT'S LIKE BLOODY BLACKPOOL ILLUMINATIONS IN HERE!" I just watch and listen to him, smile, and fill up with love and gratitude that he's my dad and I'm so lucky to have him.

"The things you take for granted someone else is praying for."

Unknown

Be Grateful and Inspired

Gratitude is the easiest way to melt away your bad energy and gear you up to being a big positive whirlwind, attracting only good into your life.

GRATITUDE BUYS YOU INSTANT HAPPINESS

Go for a walk and open your eyes. Nearly every day I walk down to the river in Richmond, North Yorkshire and the sight fills me with a sense of awe and wonder. The beautiful trees, the magnificent waterfalls, the magical birds flying in the sky and landing on the river so gracefully. It really is a magical world we live in. When you look around thinking and feeling gratitude for anything or everything then you are bringing joy, love, happiness, luck, and all things positive into your life. Even if you live in a city you can still do this. When I'm working in London I walk on the streets and look around in awe at the beautiful, amazing buildings and it inspires me as everything I see, before my eyes, was once just a thought in someone's mind which has been turned into reality for all to see. Amazing! You don't even have to go out to be filled with a sense of awe and wonder. When I'm sitting in my living room watching TV it still amazes me how the TV actually works! Then my mobile phone rings and I look at the phone thinking this phone was once just a thought in someone's mind. The human mind is incredible! When I sit on an aeroplane it amazes me how it can actually fly in the air! Don't just take anything for granted, be grateful to the people who believed in their ideas and brought them into reality for us all to enjoy and let the thought inspire you to do the same. You have the same greatness within you as everybody else, we are all children of the universe and when we are vibrating good energy, anything and everything is possible. The world is magical.

Chapter 8

The Must Have Actions to Achieve Your Dream Life

The Must Have Actions to Achieve Your Dream Life

Be The Best That You Can Be

You only get one life and one body to live it in. So make yourself the best you can possibly be in every way.

Exercise

Exercise is the best anti-depressant in the world. I find that doing exercise every day is one of the best ways to stay a happy positive whirlwind, attracting all good things to you because it raises your serotonin levels, making you feel happy. An added bonus is you will also look amazing and more people will find you attractive. You will have more energy and you will look and feel gorgeous, making you more confident in yourself! So go exercise!

Do something you enjoy, anything, as long as you are

moving your body. Join a gym, (this is also great for meeting people if you are single,) go roller skating, go walking or even do the housework to music. Do anything as long as you're active for at least an hour a day. I wake up in the morning and have my breakfast whilst reading my Dreams Come True book. Then I do an exercise DVD in my PJ's, in my bedroom. I have a shower and I am ready for the day ahead, absolutely buzzing, with my serotonin levels at a high. I attract nothing but good all day long, whilst looking and feeling good! OK, so sometimes I skip exercising, I'm not perfect. But when I forget or don't do it I can tell the difference in my daily outcome.

Diet

I hate the word diet. Nobody should ever diet. Eat a healthy option where possible, as food does affect your mood: crap food = crap mood but good food = good mood! I always eat whatever I want but only when I am hungry and I always stop when I am full. I always listen to my body and I never deny myself anything.

Physically Prepare for Success

Be Strong, Be Fit, Be Healthy, Be Gorgeous

If you deny yourself anything you want it more. This is human nature. Every time I've ever tried to diet I became obsessed with food and ate twice as much as I normally do.

So diet rules:

- ⅄ Don't diet
- ⅄ Listen to your body, if you're hungry, eat
- ⅄ When you start to feel full, stop

Ensure you are drinking enough water and keeping yourself hydrated. Thirst can often be mistaken for hunger.

When you're hungry, your body is telling you it needs fuel, your body needs fuel to function but only a certain amount of fuel, which is why you get the feeling of being full to tell you no more fuel please.

However, if you ignore your body's signal that it doesn't need any more fuel at this time and continue to fill your face then the body doesn't burn it as it already has enough fuel, so it stores it as fat!

OK so you've just had a lovely meal at a gorgeous restaurant and you were so looking forward to the gooey chocolate cake for dessert but you feel full after your main course, you could eat the dessert there and then and end up wearing it on your bum, legs and tum or you could ask for a take-out piece of cake and wait until your body gives you the sign that it needs fuel again.

i.e. You feel hungry and eat it and not end up wearing it as your body actually needs to burn it for fuel.

So you're not on a diet, you can eat whatever you feel like eating but ONLY WHEN YOU ARE HUNGRY AND STOP WHEN YOU ARE FULL

I have had three children and my body is the same as it was in my modeling days, well, apart from my potatoes in socks boobs, haha! I am the same weight and same size, so I get a lot of people asking me do I have any diet tips.

My Diet Tips =

- Eat when hungry
- Stop when full
- Only drink still water, black coffee, green tea
- Don't deny yourself any food if you are hungry, you can eat whatever you like

- No soda!

- Alcohol no more than once a week at the very most

- Take acai berry tablets – they have lots of health benefits and are classed as a superfood but they also suppress the appetite, so naturally aid you in weight loss and make your skin lovely as well.

- Take raspberry ketone tablets. Raspberry ketone causes the fat within your cells to be broken up more effectively, helping your body burn fat faster.

- Get busy achieving your dreams. Nothing causes overeating like sitting around being bored. Get up and take steps towards your dream.

Water

A rule I swear by is drinking 2 litres of water every day to keep all of your organs, skin and brain in tip top condition. Water gives you energy and you will never have a dehydration headache or constipation when you drink enough water. Water is also a miracle worker for your looks. It helps with giving you clear beautiful skin and, if you have wrinkles, it plumps them away and makes your eyes clear and sparkly. Get drinking water and get all sparkly again!

Make the Most of Yourself

Be clean and tidy from your kitchen to your bikini line. When everything about you and your life is clean, clear and tidy, it makes your mind clean, clear and tidy. In my experience it somehow seems to help the universe deliver all of your dreams.

Give your house a spring clean, chuck out all the clutter and anything you don't need - give to charity. A clear house = a clear mind! It will make you feel happier, more peaceful and more motivated. Never underestimate just being clean and tidy.

Give your body a spring clean; exfoliate all dead skin cells to reveal new glowing ones. Have a manicure and a pedicure. There is no excuse to have scruffy chipped nail varnish when you can get a manicure or do it yourself, cheaply, at home. If you want the job of your dreams it's better to look your best at all times to give off the impression you respect and look after yourself. Have a full body wax or shave everywhere if you are a wimp like me. Give your hair a conditioning treatment; you can do this yourself at home for very little cost. Have a colonic irrigation if you can; a colonic irrigation is basically a tube up your bum which washes your system out. I swear by these, as it makes me feel lighter, my stomach is flatter and it makes my skin amazing and glowing. Also, I never have spots if I have regular colonic irrigations.

Wear make up to accentuate what you have. Get a haircut and hair colour that suits you. Ditch the black clothes for well-fitting colourful ones that lift your mood. If you have great legs then show them off! If you have a great cleavage, make the most of it with a lovely top. The better you look, the better you will feel and the more confident you will feel. Put effort into how you look, you deserve it! As I've already said, you only get one life and one body to lead it with, so make the most of yourself and be the best that you can possibly be.

Be Nice! Be Nice! Be Nice!

Be nice to everybody. When you are friendly to people then people are friendly back. You get back what you give out.

"It's nice to be important but more important to be nice"

John Cassis

Wherever you go, whoever you meet, only see the good in people and be nice to them. It is always important to remember people's names and to take an interest in them. Smile at everybody and be nice to everybody and see your world become beautiful and friendly.

Never slag anybody off. Never be unkind or belittle anybody because when you do that you are only hurting yourself. It doesn't look or sound nice when you see people being unkind. It's very unattractive and it will make the people listening to you be wary of you and not trust you to not do the same to them. Remember, if you have nothing nice to say then don't say anything at all!

I know it's hard but try to send the negative individuals love and appreciate them as well. Look for the good in them. They are only human, with the same thoughts, insecurities and love to give - as the rest of us. If you label a friend, boss or stranger a complete muppet or bitch, that's how you will always see them and what you will always expect of them because that's always been your experience of them. So that is what you are going to keep getting if you don't give everyone a fresh start every time you meet them. Be and feel kind and warm towards them and look for the good in them.

Then you will see a big difference. That bitch just might roll over for you to tickle its tummy instead of snarling at you.

GIVE OUT BAD, GET BAD BACK.

GIVE OUT GOOD, GET GOOD BACK.

Look for and see the good in everybody, even if you haven't been able to stand them in the past. Your negative thoughts toward them are only hurting you, nobody else. So only see, think and feel good about people. If you really can't do this, then avoid the person.

Fill Up Your World

Most people want to have it all. Having it all is harder work but it brings confidence and independence which gives you an inner glow, you feel stronger and more powerful.

This is my world

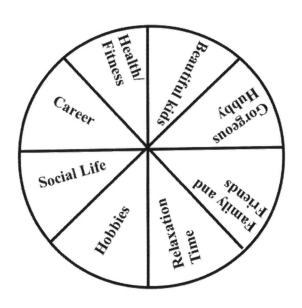

Life is full of ups and downs. It's how you deal withthem that matters. I believe that with a full life, if a slice of your world goes wrong, say you split up with your partner, you still have all the other slices to give you security and keep you busy whilst you're down.

I had a client who shall remain nameless, who met the man of her dreams and moved away with him. He told her she didn't need to work again which she thought was brilliant so she moved away leaving her friends, family and career behind her. Her world then looked like this.

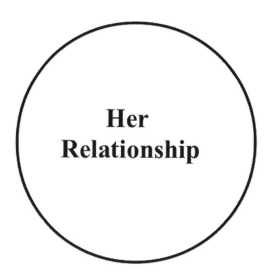

Her Relationship

She sat in her new home waiting for her man to come home every day and was upset when he came in late from work, as she had been on her own all day. This is turn started to bug the man of her dreams as he had fallen in love with a confident, independent fun-loving girl who was always coming and going. She had now become a nag who was always there waiting for him, so the arguments began and eventually the man of her dreams had had enough and ended the relationship. o this now left her world like this:

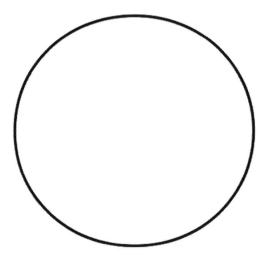

So of course because she didn't have the security of all the other fulfilled slices of her life she was in a very sad place.

The moral of the story: keep your life full and when you meet the man of your dreams it is even more important to keep busy with your fulfilled life so you stay strong, powerful and confident!

This applies to every aspect of your life. I had another client who only focused on her career. She worked every single hour God sent, so when she had a bad day at the office it hit her hard and she went home to her lovely flat on her own and mulled it over and over in her head all night.

Her Career

However if she had a full life, partner, family, friends and hobbies, she wouldn't have time to sit there feeling sorry for herself, her full little world would give her the perspective to appreciate that it was just a bad day at the office, plus a cuddle from a boyfriend wouldn't hurt either!

Make an effort with friends and family, join a gym get yourself out there, you can't meet new people if you never take the plunge and go to new places. Push yourself out of your comfort zone, try a new hobby each week or month, you never know where it might lead. If you want the man of your dreams, are you going to the right places? Get on the internet, try out an online dating site, it's all the rage these days.

Get Things Done – Take Action

So we're on the right track to getting things done. We're going to take action and get organised.

Get up Early!

The early bird catches the worm and all that jazz. I came across how getting up early is good for you from an inspirational page on Twitter, which tweeted that people who get up every day at 7am are skinnier and happier. I hadn't been getting up early until I read this,

I'd been sleeping in until 9 or 10, sometimes even 11, and after all those hours of sleep I felt dreadful. I felt sluggish, weak and tired. So I thought, well let's put their tweet to the test and decided to try getting up at 7am every day, even at the weekend. The first few days were difficult as my body wasn't used to it, it just wanted to go back to bed. But by day 3 I began to notice the benefits:

- I was up!
- I had my breakfast in peace and quiet before my mad family woke up
- I got my housework done
- I was washed and dressed when the kids woke up
- I had more energy
- I was up and at 'em
- I was happier and yes, I think skinnier

Now if by 7am you are already on the tube, in your car or at work, then just try waking up an hour earlier than your normal time and get a few little jobs done that you wouldn't normally get done, even if it's a bit of brekky and read a few positive quotes before you do the dishes, then leisurely get ready for work instead of rushing! See how much better it feels.

To Do List

Every morning either when you get to work or when you get home from dropping the kids off at nursery, write your daily to do list of things that need to be done that day. Mine normally goes something like this:

- Go to the gym
- An hour of writing on the book I'm working on
- Housework
- Food shopping
- Cook dinner
- Pick kids up
- Washing
- Quality time with my hubby and kids

Once I have finished my list I look at it and sometimes if I have had a busy day I know I'm not going to get all that done so I decide which ones to do and which ones won't matter if I don't get round to them. Ask yourself which tasks on your list could affect your life in a positive way the most. Here's what I decided:

Gym – It will affect my future because exercise today, fit and hot bod tomorrow. If I exercise today I will raise my serotonin levels and be in a good mood and attract good things and have good actions, so I have decided that I will do this, even if it's only half an hour.

An hour of writing – This could affect my future life in a positive light as it may end up published. It's also raising my self-esteem as I'm working on my passion and purpose in life – I will definitely do this task.

Housework – This will not affect my future in any way apart from tidy house, tidy mind, so I will leave this until tomorrow as I don't have time today.

Food shopping – If I don't do this today it won't impact my future so I'll leave this today. We can make do with the food we have in the cupboards.

Cook dinner – Obviously a homemade healthy dinner for the family and myself is preferable. But you can find healthy option takeaways and ready meals for busy families, these days. so not today.

Pick kids up – Errr well I would say this is very important, haha, but if you get the chance, delegate, but if I have no one today I'll be doing this task.

Washing – No chance. I haven't got time and it won't affect my future, so not today.

Quality time with my family and hubby – If you want a happy family in the future then quality time together every day is a must. Even if it's just all sitting down for a meal together.

So now you have halved your to do list, you have taken the pressure off yourself so you have time and energy to do the important stuff.

Act as if You Already Are What You Want to be

If you're a shy person, lacking in self-confidence, go out and act as if you are amazingly confident until this is your natural state. That is exactly what I did years ago when I was a teenager. I was so shy I wouldn't even go in a shop without someone with me in case I had to ask for something. I also used to lack confidence in myself. I used to shake with nerves just thinking about having to speak to a stranger or being somewhere I didn't know anybody and I believed I would always be like that. Luckily I went on to learn that life doesn't have to be a nerve-wracking struggle. I changed my belief from I am shy to I am amazingly confident in all situations.

When I believed I was shy I was once in a club in Blackpool and a modelling agency approached me and asked me to enter the Miss Blackpool competition. Before I could answer my mum said, "Yes, she will do it!" I was shaking with fear but I managed to get through to the finals. When the day of the final arrived I was filled with dread at the thought of what lay ahead. I had to walk on stage in front of 400 people in swimwear, then daywear, then evening wear and when I was in my evening wear I had to walk to the front of the stage and say a little bit about myself: my name, my occupation, my hopes and dreams for the future etc. I walked on in my red sequin dress and I was shaking with fear. I got to the microphone and froze. No words would come out of my mouth, I managed to mumble my name was Tanya then ran off the stage mortified. I was completely embarrassed and annoyed that I had let a little belief that I was desperately shy and lacking in confidence ruin my life. I thought that's it! Enough's enough! I am not shy or lacking in confidence any more. I AM AMAZINGLY CONFIDENT IN ALL SITUATIONS! Of course I was still shy inside but from that day on, everything I did, everywhere I went, and everybody who I spoke to, I did so acting and pretending, as if I was amazingly confident. Eventually I wasn't acting or pretending any more because my new belief was my new reality. I wanted to try out my new belief the following year by entering Miss Blackpool again and guess what? I won! The desperately shy me who had run off the stage the year before had gone back and won the competition just by changing a simple thought. I've never been shy since.

This works in all situations. Change all your negative thoughts and beliefs to positive new ones then act or pretend as if they are true until they become your reality.

FAKE IT TILL YOU MAKE IT!

Change Your Daily Routine to Success

"If you keep doing what you've always done you, you'll keep getting what you've always got."
W L Bateman

Now that you know and have all the tools to go and get and live your dream life, you need to incorporate them into your life, they need to be added to your daily routine.

I was half-way through writing my first self-help book, I wanted so much to have my book published and finished to share with the world the secrets I have learnt so that people can live their dream life as I am doing. But for some reason I was finding it hard to finish the book and I didn't know how I was going to get it published for people to read. This was very worrying to me as I was a life coach writing a book on how to get what you want, but at this moment in time I wasn't getting what I wanted.

Then it dawned on me that I had been so busy living my dream life that I had forgotten to do what I always preach to my clients, so I began to write a diary and went back to basics. I had to change my daily routine to get what I wanted.

Everyday Daily Routine

- Get up early

- Meditate and imagine living your dream

- Exercise 30 minutes

- Read Dreams to Reality book

- Look at vision board, visualise and feel like you already have everything on your vision board in your life today.

- Drink 2.5 litres of water

- Take one action towards your dream

(Even if it's something as small as making a phone call)

- Act as if you are what you want to be
(Fake it until you make it)

Chapter 9

Don't Become Desperate For Anything or Anyone

Don't Become Desperate For Anything or Anyone

Wanting something or someone too desperately is not good. It's very negative energy and when you become negative energy you will never attract what you want. Now I might sound like I'm contradicting myself here because I have been telling you to think about and imagine what it is that you want because your most dominant thoughts become your reality. You do need to do this. But not in a needy desperate way. The tighter you try to hold on to something that you really want or are afraid of losing, or of not getting it at all, results in you pushing it further away from you. Being desperate or needy or both comes from feeling fearful. But relax and remember you have nothing to fear as no matter what happens things will always turn out perfectly in the end. I'll give you a couple of examples:

Let's say all you really want is to settle down with the man of your dreams, but you're single. Your positive thinking brings you a date with someone you think you could really like and the date goes amazingly well. You think this person could actually be the one because they tick all of your boxes. You get excited and hone in on this person because you want it to work so badly, but then they don't call or text when you want them to. They don't invite you on a night out when you know that everybody else is taking their partner. You end up getting all desperate and needy thinking he's the one so why is he not treating me like the one? That's because he might not be the one, maybe this person has been sent to practise your dating skills until the real man of your dreams comes along. Perhaps he could be the one but you have become so desperate to have him you have turned needy and are giving out negative energy which is pushing him away. CHILL OUT! CALM DOWN AND RELAX! You have asked for, imagined and thought about your perfect partner and you will receive him/her when the time is right and if you stay a happy whirlwind of good energy. Let's face it, DESPERATE AIN'T SEXY! So open your mind and trust, you don't have to do anything but stay positive and patient. If not him then it's because someone better is on their way. You will notice that when you are happy within yourself and trust that you will get what you want when the time is right, then all the neediness and desperation disappears, making you irresistible to the opposite sex.

The same goes for your work life. Let's say you are a singer wanting a record deal. You have been thinking about, writing about and imagining the end result: you as a famous singer, singing in front of millions of people with your album in the shops. Just a tip from past experience, I did exactly this but I only imagined the middle bit and not the end result, I got a record deal at the first meeting, at the first record company I went to and my album was in the shops and I got loads of press. However I wasn't specific in how the record would perform, I didn't think about it, write about or imagine my album selling or people actually listening or enjoying it. That's the most important part because no one listening to your music, reading your writing, enjoying your art or whatever your chosen career path may be = no success. So make sure you think about, write about and imagine that as well. Imagine circumstances where you end up meeting a record company but instead of staying positive you start to want it to go so well that you become nervous, then you become doubtful about your abilities and start thinking things like, "Oh my God, if I don't get this it's over for me, this is my last chance." Having thoughts like this and dwelling on them instead of dismissing them makes you become desperate. People can smell desperation, which is not good because desperation is a very negative energy.

NEGATIVE THOUGHTS = NEGATIVE FEELINGS = NEGATIVE ENERGY = NEGATIVE ACTIONS = NEGATIVE REALITY!

Negative energy can only result in a negative outcome so change your mind set. Dismiss negative thoughts and only think positive thoughts and imagine the end result as you want it to be. It doesn't matter if this record company, college or firm doesn't take you on because if you are staying positive you will get something better. This meeting might have been a learning curve for you to give you experience or get a new contact for your real break, or this might actually be your break, so there's nothing to lose either way. The key is to never make any circumstance and especially any person the reason for happiness. Trust that if you can't have the thing or person you want then it's because something better awaits you, so just relax and enjoy the journey to your dreams.

"Success is not the way to happiness, happiness is the way to success."
Herman Cain

"I have learnt more from my failures than my successes."
Richard Branson

I always remember moaning to my best friend Kitty about my bad luck one day and she told me this story I'm about to share with you that her dad told her.

GOOD LUCK BAD LUCK!

There is a Chinese story of a farmer who used an old horse to till his fields. One day the horse escaped into the hills and when the neighbours sympathised with the old man over his bad luck, the farmer replied, "Bad luck? Good luck? Who knows?" A week later, the horse returned with a herd of horses from the hills and this time the neighbours congratulated the farmer on his good luck. His reply was, "Good luck? Bad luck? Who knows?"

Then, when the farmer's son was attempting to tame one of the wild horses, he fell off its back and broke his leg. Everyone thought this was very bad luck. Not the farmer, whose only reaction was, "Bad luck? Good luck? Who knows?"

Some weeks later, the army marched into the village and conscripted every able bodied youth they found there. When they found the farmer's son with his broken leg, they let him off. Now was that bad luck or good luck?

Who knows?

Everything that seems on the surface to be an evil may be a good in disguise. And everything that seems good on the surface may really be an evil. So we are wise when we leave it to life to decide what good fortune is and what is misfortune and be thankful and trust that all things turn out for good with those who love life.

Author unknown

Chapter 10

Putting Things into Perspective

Putting Things into Perspective

Putting Things into Perspective

Sometimes shit happens. You may have attracted it into your life by your negative thinking or it may be down to someone/thing else outside your control. You can control yourself but you can't control others, so sometimes shit happens. That's life but what you can control is how you deal with it and how you deal with it is what counts.

Your partner cheats on you. Your best friend has said unkind things behind your back because she is jealous of your new look confident self. Someone physically harms you. Your roof falls in after bad weather. The list of bad things that could happen is endless so the first thing you need to do is sit down, calm down and breathe. Ask yourself: this time next year will this really matter? I am still alive so is it actually a big deal? You can't control others or some circumstances but you can control how you deal with them. You have the choice of whether you want it to send you into a depression, make you sad, bitter, angry and full of hatred, making you very bad energy, which is only going to attract more bad things to you. OR you can simply say - you know what? Life is too short to waste my time feeling bad about this. Decide what you want to do about the situation (whatever you do, make your decision when you are in a good positive mood because you can never solve a problem whilst being negative and there is a chance of making the situation worse. Make sure you have calmed down and got yourself in a better mood before deciding what to do). Then, when you have decided, forgive the person/

yourself/ circumstance that has caused the temporary shit blip in your life and carry on loving and appreciating your life and everybody in it.

I love the saying "God will not take you to what he cannot pull you through." I also love the 'Putting things into perspective' exercise by Dr Tony Clarke-Holland;

*Have I died? - NO

*Has my head fallen off? - NO

*Is what happened to me history? - YES

*Can I decide what happens next? - MOST DEFINITELY!

*Can anyone else take away my dreams? - NO

*Do I still have the capacity to love and share? - YOU BET!

*Am I feeling more positive about my future already?

-YES!

*Can I continue to put large and small things into perspective going forward? - COURSE YOU CAN!

Now chill out, breath and stop taking yourself and your life so seriously. You are as happy as you decide to be. The past has gone and there is nothing you can do about it so forget it, forgive and take the chip off your shoulder and decide to be a success story despite what's happened to you in the past. You only get one life so enjoy it. Sometimes God or the universe or your guardian angel (whoever that is for you) clears things in your life or doesn't give you what you want because something far better is waiting for you. For example, let's say you have been being really positive then all of a sudden your boyfriend dumps you! What's happening? It might be that the universe is making way for a better model to come into your life who makes you happier. Or maybe it's best that you and your boyfriend part for a while so that you both appreciate what you had together so that when you get back together it's a new, improved, loving relationship.

You are strong and powerful

Always remember that you are strong and powerful. You have what it takes to get through everything and anything. Life won't take you to what it can't pull you through. No matter who you are, you are strong and powerful. You might feel weak sometimes but that is only because you are thinking weak thoughts. Dismiss those weak thoughts because you CAN handle anything and everything! You might think "That's rubbish, I couldn't handle it if this happened or if that happened," but that's just your mind bullshit talking.

Even if your worst nightmare did happen to you, you would get through it no matter what! So when you ignore your mind bullshit and think I can and will get through anything, no matter what, watch your worry and fear dissolve.

"Expose yourself to your deepest fear, after that fear has no power, you are free"
Jim Morrison

You have to keep practising this because the first couple of times your mind bullshit will keep throwing lots of bullshit thoughts into your mind like "Oh my God, but what if this happens or that happens," but just stay calm and recognise that it's only your mind bullshit having a party again. Smile to yourself and think I CAN AND WILL GET THROUGH ANYTHING AND EVERYTHING, NO MATTER WHAT! Then get back to living your life to the full and achieving your dreams.

Chapter 11

Take Action

Take Action

"The best way to predict the future is to create it."
Abraham Lincoln

Take Action

Whatever you do in this present moment could improve your future. There's nothing to make you feel more positive than ending a day feeling like you've done something that's taken you a step closer to your dream. What could you do in this present moment that could take you a step closer to achieving your dream?

You achieve your dreams the same as you build a house, brick by brick. The bricks are goals and goals are like the little stepping stones to reach our dreams. Once you have decided what your dream is you need to set little achievable goals to reach your dream. Your dream needs to excite you or you might struggle with having enough motivation to follow through to achieve it. So make sure your dream excites you and makes you feel enthusiastic and alive.

It's no good only wishing, dreaming and hoping for your dreams to come true. You've been positive thinking about, imagining and writing about your dream, so now your dream is in motion to come to you, bringing positive circumstances and opportunities which could come in any way, shape or form. You could meet someone who has a really good contact who could help you. Or you happen to read a book or a newspaper article which gives you information you need. Or a friend asks you out and you end up meeting someone. The list of possibilities is endless but when this does happen - TAKE ACTION! Just like I did when I sent my pictures off to FHM after I saw the advert in the paper. If I hadn't taken action at that time then my dream wouldn't have become my reality. Thankfully I did take action and I achieved my dream.

TAKE ACTION NOW! GO FOR IT! YOU CAN EASILY DO IT! NO EXCUSES! Just go for it and take all the steps needed to achieve your dreams, you will be glad you did.

You can have lots of different dreams: one for your career, one for your love life, your social life etc. You can have as many dreams as you wish but make sure they are your dreams not somebody else's, because your dreams have to excite you and make you feel alive or you will never have the motivation to achieve them.

It has been proven time and time again that people, who plan, are more successful, so plan! What little actions do you need to take to achieve the goals that will generate your dream? Who do you need to contact? Do you need to research? Do you need to join a college or a gym? Or sign up for singing lessons or acting lessons? It could even be that your dream is to have a nice smile because you are conscious of your yellow crooked teeth. Well if that's the case write down some goals that will help you achieve your dream smile, like save money and book a consultation with a dentist. If you don't like something, from your job to your teeth, change it, fix it, you have the power to do anything. Write down what actions you need to take in order to achieve the goals needed to reach your dream.

"Anything is possible if you've got enough nerve." J K. Rowling

MY DREAM

IS: ....

....

THE STEPS I NEED TO TAKE TO REACH MY DREAM ARE:

Step 1.

My first step is to:

I can easily achieve step 1 because:

I will complete step 1 by the following date:

Completing step 1 will make me feel:

Tick when the step is complete

Step 2.

My second step is to:

I can easily achieve step 2 because:

I will complete step 2 by the following date:

Completing step 2 will make me feel:

Tick when the step is complete

Step 3.

My third step is to:

Things I need to do to achieve this step:

I can easily achieve step 3 because:

I will complete step 3 by the following date:

Completing step 3 will make feel:

Tick when the step is complete

Step 4.

My fourth step is to:

Things I need to do to achieve this step:

I can easily achieve step 4 because:

I will complete step 4 by the following date:

Completing step 4 will make me feel:

Tick when the step is complete

Step 5.

My fifth step is to:

Things I need to do to achieve this step:

I can easily achieve step 5 because:

I will complete step 5 by the following date:

Completing step 5 will make me feel:

Tick when the step is complete

I HAVE ACHIEVED MY DREAM

You may need to take more steps: you can add as many as you like. I always put little boxes at the end of each step that you can tick when completed. When you have completed a step towards your dream, doing that little tick gives you a great sense of achievement and increased self-confidence. Be proud of yourself for every tick. Well done!

Don't tell anybody about your steps and dreams just in case they say something to dent your confidence or make you doubt that your dreams are attainable. Some people don't like it when other people are trying to better themselves and their lives as it makes them feel inferior or worried that you might leave them behind. So it's best to keep your steps and ideas to yourself and only tell people who you need to help you and people who you know will be positive and build you up and support you. Everybody else will know about your dream when you have achieved it. You will easily achieve it so go do it!

Now for those of you who have not just written down your goals and steps to action, this next bit is for you.

Procrastination

Pro.cras.ti.nate [proh-kras-tuh-neyt, pruh-] verb,

pro.cras.ti.nat.ed, pro.cras.ti.nat.ing.

(used without object)

✂️ 🗎🗎🗎 to defer action; delay: to procrastinate until an opportunity is lost.

It's very common to procrastinate over things, and this trait usually goes back a long way. I don't know about you but no matter how long I had to complete my homework I would always complete it the night before it was due in, or on the way to school, and because it was rushed, it was crap and made me feel crap. When you complete any task/project you get a great feeling of satisfaction and pride. Completing any task or project etc. increases your confidence and self-esteem levels.

Even just making a start on a task feels so rewarding, and you wonder why you didn't start it sooner.

Yet so many people still procrastinate and make excuses for not getting on and doing it. WHY?

I believe the number one reason is because the task seems so big that it's unachievable and harder than they think, and maybe before teachers dish out big projects and homework they should think about this. But this goes for any task we come up against in life.
Cut it up into manageable pieces.
If you put pressure on yourself and give yourself a deadline to complete something, it gives you a sense of urgency. Cut things down into small pieces and do little bits, one a day and you'll find that when you complete one little step you will feel so energised and

satisfied that you will want to carry on and do another and another and then before you know it you will have achieved your dream and be on cloud nine.

Whilst writing this book I had to make each chapter longer as I'm very straight to the point and can say everything I want to say in a few words. However that doesn't bode well for a book apparently, so I agreed to develop each chapter further, but this seemed like a mammoth task.

I kept putting it off, I cut it down into little steps so that it didn't seem so scary, the first step being to pick up a pen and paper.

It's also important to get yourself into the right frame of mind before you start on a task. It's essential to push away any self-limiting beliefs which may pop into your head, e.g. I'm not good enough, I can't do it, what if I fail, what's the point? Once you get rid of these then you'll have a clear mind to get focused on the task in hand. It's also good to have a little think about how you'll feel if you don't complete the task. Angry with yourself... frustrated... annoyed... tense... like the weight of the world is on your shoulders. Visualise the joy and elation you'll feel when you've completed the task, and how good that will make you feel.

Thoughts of a procrastinator on her dissertation – Kitty:

My dissertation was a massive source of procrastination I couldn't see how I'd ever be able to write 10,000 words on anything, never mind the subject I'd opted for which believe it or not was factors in motivation! I procrastinated for ages and at times felt like giving up. But I kept plugging away at it, doing a little bit more and a little bit more. Eventually it all started coming together, and the sheer elation I felt when I handed it in was amazing. I'd completed it and handed it in on time, I knew that I'd done my best and that was all that mattered. It felt so good.

Sometimes all it takes is for you to start achieving your goal is to get your equipment. For example:
Losing weight – Put your gym gear and trainers on
Writing a book – Pick up a pen and paper
Making a call, whether it be to sell something, or ask someone out on a date – Go to a quiet room and make that call

Once you make the first move in the right direction it gets the momentum going and there'll be no stopping you.

I just did this about 20 minutes ago, I picked up a pen and paper and told myself I was going to do 10 minutes of free writing for this book. I picked up a pen and paper and started writing and even when my 10 minutes was up, I couldn't stop. Twenty minutes of writing has now passed and I'm still here writing and loving it. I feel so energised and happy.

Sometimes you've got to just do it. Do it! Do it now! Get your pen, your laptop out, get your trainers on or pick up the phone, whatever it is you've been wanting to do, now is the time to start! DO IT NOW!

Once you start and you're motivated, keep going while you're on a roll. If you start and keep going and complete the job in hand, not only will you feel on top of the world but you will save yourself so much time in the long run. You'll remember how much time it took you to motivate yourself to start working last time! So keep going! No excuses!

Preparation and opportunity = luck

If you want to be lucky in life, lucky in your career, lucky in love. You have to do the preparation first. If you want to have a number one best-selling book – write a number one best-selling book. If you want to be lucky in love, then be the best you can be (see chapter 8). So when the opportunity knocks on the door and you open it to find Prince Charming standing there, you'll be gorgeous, confident and ready for him to work at sweeping you off your feet.

So don't procrastinate do all the preparation, no matter what that may be or you will kick yourself if a big opportunity arises and you're just not ready. What a waste that would be. Don't kick yourself, just get to work.

Even when you think you are fully prepared, do more! When the opportunity arises you may have competition and the last thing you want is to watch someone else who was more prepared than you walk away with the prize you want. There will always be room for improvement and you should never close your mind to anything and always keep learning to stay ahead.

Ants can lift 50 times their own weight

Crappy little jobs like posting a letter, making a phone call, tidying the house, taking the bins out, sorting receipts for a tax return or cleaning the car out are the ones which take time from your day. They take up space in your mind which in turn distracts you from the major tasks you actually want to get cracking with. Get the little tasks done and ticked off your list, this will free your mind and give you the space to start dealing with the big things. I get great satisfaction from writing a list of things to do, working through them and ticking them off one by one.

Sometimes the big mountain of a task - the one that's the scariest and hardest to start – can be put off for longer and longer by the tiny distractions – mini tasks.

Sometimes we go out of our way to avoid the thing that we really want to do. Fear is a major factor in putting things off, but what you need to think about is, what's the worst that can happen if you do get cracking and climb that mountain? It's worth having a go...

"Only those who risk going too far, will find out how far they can possibly go."
T.S. Elliot

Clear out the negative thinking and just do it!

What is it that you're putting off doing? Think about the reasons why you're not getting cracking and getting it done.

Chapter 12

Expect, Listen, Receive and Enjoy

Expect, Listen, Receive and Enjoy

Expect, Listen and Receive

It is important to always expect your dreams to come true. Once you expect something it will come. However, if you're not expecting your dreams to become your reality because of your lack of belief, then they are either not going to turn up at all or when they do you'll miss them. Don't let your perfect future pass you by because you are not looking out for the signs that are telling you to take action to get your dream. I started to believe that one day I could be a model and expected it to happen so when I opened the newspaper and saw the advert looking for the next cover girl for FHM magazine I knew it was a sign that I had to take action.

Let's say your dream is to find a new partner but you're having no luck when your friend tells you about a dating site she went on which was brilliant. Well, that could be a sign to join up, your dream partner could be there waiting to ask you out. The best way to look out for and receive your dream is to always pay attention to your gut instinct. If you get a gut instinct to do something that feels good, then do it! I had a strong feel-good, excited, gut instinct to send my pictures to FHM as soon as I saw the advert. My dream of becoming a model came true through paying attention to that gut instinct. However, equally if you have a gut instinct not to do something, then don't do it. I always remember having a strong gut feeling not to do a topless photo shoot. I had been modelling for 5 years and I had always turned down topless work. I always wore at least a bra or had my hands covering my

185

boobies in all of my photos but because I kept on turning down the topless work, over the years the magazines kept offering me more and more money to do it. A few of the newspapers had published pictures of me sunbathing topless on holiday and I was still a single mum and needed the money so I thought well I might as well do it because people have seen my breasts anyway, I might as well just do it to get the money. So I ignored my gut instinct telling me that this doesn't feel right and not to do it. I went ahead and did the topless shoot and every time I see a topless photograph of myself it makes me cringe. It is one of the biggest regrets of my life and from that experience I have learnt the hard way to always listen to my gut instinct.

If it feels good - go with it. If it feels a bit dodgy or

not quite right or something's telling you not to do it or not to go there - it's your gut instinct. Learn to listen to it. It's always right.

Do not get caught up in how what you want is going to come to you, just carry on imagining the end result of what you want. Life will figure out the ins and outs of how your dream will come to you, your only job is to feel good, positive and grateful about what you already have around you. When you think of your dream, feel excited and feel the good happy positive feelings you would feel if it were already here. All the things you are thinking about and imagining in your mind you will receive as your reality so it is very important to concentrate onwhat you want and not what you don't want.

"If you see it in your mind you will hold it in your hand."Bob Proctor

It is important to look out for the signs of your dream being delivered to you. You might get a feeling to go somewhere or contact someone. It may not always arrive as you expect it to, look out for all good coincidences. They are normally how your dreams are delivered to you. Many people ask for a certain thing and then give up because they think it doesn't work but it is working, they are just missing the signs.

A woman lived in a beautiful valley next to the river. One day the rain was so bad the river burst its banks and flooded the whole valley. The water quickly rose up and up, the woman climbed up into her attic for safety and asked God to save her and believed he would save her. Sometime later a rescue boat arrived and the life guard shouted through her window, "Come with us." But the woman replied, "No, it's ok, God will save me." The water was getting higher and higher when another rescue boat arrived but again the woman sent it away saying, "God will save me." By this point the water was up to her shoulders and she was freezing, when a third rescue boat came along and tried really hard to convince the woman to get into the boat but she refused as she was sure that God would save her. The rescue boat had no choice but to leave her and soon after the woman drowned. When she arrived in heaven she said to God, "Why didn't you save me?" and God replied, "I sent you 3 boats, what more do you want?"

What you think about and imagine always comes to you, if you believe you can have or achieve it and feel good when you think of it. However, it may come in a different form or repackaged differently to how you imagined it. The best piece of advice I ever received was - whilst you are waiting for your dream to become your reality, look at what you already have and feel love and appreciation for everything and everyone who already exists in your life. This will bring your dreams and your positive reality to you far more quickly, whilst making every day of your life more enjoyable.

Everyone can lead their dream life, especially you! So what are you waiting for? Go get it!

Chapter 13

A Wee Recap

A Wee Recap

Here's a little recap for any forgetful dory out there :-)

Don't get bitter, get better!
Remember it's not time that heals it's your mindset. If you decide you are better, watch yourself get better!

You are what you think.
Negative thoughts = negative feelings = negative actions = negative reality!
So always ignore negative thoughts and think of positive alternatives.
Positive thoughts = positive feelings = positive actions = positive reality!

All negative thoughts are mind bullshit.

Don't let your mind run wild, control it! Ignore negative thoughts and think positive. Remember, worry is just misuse of imagination and almost all of what you worry about never happens, so don't waste your time on it. Life is far too short.

Get rid of those limiting beliefs about yourself.

You can be and do anything you want! Fake it till you make it and remember the sky is absolutely NOT the limit! There's a whole universe out there!

What do you want?

How can you get what you want if you don't know what it is? Define and refine what you want, then think about it, write about it and imagine having it.

Preparation is the key to success!

If you fail to plan then you plan to fail!

Preparation + Opportunity = Luck

Keep checking your attitude is one that's taking you towards your dream life.

Stay positive, be happy, smile, love and appreciate everyone and everything. Be grateful and inspired. Gratitude buys you instant happiness.

Exercise is the best anti-depressant in the world!

Get exercising it'll increase your serotonin levels and will make you feel amazing.

Don't diet.

If you are hungry, eat! If you are full, stop! If you are not hungry then don't eat, even if you are in a restaurant.

Fill up your world.
Then if a part of it goes wrong, it's not the end of your world!

Get up early.
That early bird always catches those worms.

Act as if you already are who you want to be.
This is the quickest way to becoming who you want to be. Play. Make. Believe.

Don't become desperate for anything or anyone.
Remember, desperate isn't sexy.

Always put things into perspective.

Will this actually matter in five years' time? Has your head fallen off or have you died?

Take Action! Don't Procrastinate!

Take action and you will feel amazing once you have. No excuses, just go for it!

Always expect your dreams to come true.

Always listen to your gut instinct. If it feels good, do it. If something feels bad or off, then don't do it.

You are amazing!

You are so much stronger and powerful than you can ever imagine. You can easily achieve your dreams.

Conclusion

You now have all the tools and techniques you need to go and create your dream life, you are absolutely good enough and capable of achieving anything you want in life. If you start to doubt yourself just re-read relevant bits in the book. You can do this!

Go go go!

May all your dreams become your reality.

All my love and best wishes

Tanya Bardo

Dream to Reality Bracelets

by Tanya Bardo

Available at www.tanyabardo.com

Dreams to reality bracelets have been created by Tanya Bardo to help turn your dreams to reality. Every bracelet comes with a set of instructions. Please follow the instructions and complete the exercises before putting the bracelet on.

Each bracelet has been lovingly made by hand in a cosy North East studio by jewellery designer Emma Hedley, healing harp music is played throughout the process ensuring lots of love and positive energy has been sealed into each and every one of the dreams to reality bracelets.

The exclusive angel wing design was created with five feathers on the wing to act as a daily reminder for you to take action and put the steps in place to work towards making your dreams come true.

Cast in solid sterling silver with pure twisted silk chord. An ideal gift for a loved one or even a treat for yourself.

Unisex bracelets available in two sizes Small or Large.

Struggling to decide which colour bracelet to go for? Here's some information on colour symbolism which might help you make your mind up.

Red – excitement, energy, passion and love

Silver – security, reliability, intelligence and calm

Black – power, elegance, wealth and protection

May all your dreams become your reality! xxx

Notes

Notes

Notes

Notes

Notes

Notes

Notes

Printed in Great Britain
by Amazon.co.uk, Ltd.,
Marston Gate.